KNOW
- YOUR -
WORTH,
GIRL

Dr. Marilou Ryder
Jessica Thompson

Know Your Worth, Girl
Invest in Yourself and Spend it on You! Inspirations, Hints, Tips and Truths

COPYRIGHT © 2020 Marilou Ryder and Jessica Thompson

Paperback ISBN: 978-0-9904103-8-6
Kindle: 978-0-9904103-9-3
Library of Congress Control Number: 2020944873

Printed in the United States of America
Delmar Publishing, Huntington Beach, CA 92648

KNOW
- YOUR -
WORTH,
GIRL

Who is smarter, prettier, and wore it better?
Not us! We are all getting to the finish line!

INTRODUCTION

K*now Your Worth, Girl.* Have you ever thought about it? Not just in monetary terms but as a female living your life. As authors and women advocates, we believe that knowing who you are and showing your worth in society is very important while navigating life successfully. That is why we want you to recognize your worth and start to invest in it. We believe that knowing how to manage your worth and increase its daily value will ultimately make you more confident, courageous and powerful in your environment.

We are delighted to pass on to you a few of our favorite investment categories. We'd like to introduce you to our 30-Day Challenge to encourage you to step outside of your comfort zone. We challenge you with 30 days of tasks that will strengthen your ability to achieve your worth. After all, we all know, "Life begins at the edge of our Comfort Zone". See if you can stay the course and challenge yourself.

Another focus on knowing your worth is to identify with other women who show their worth every day. Enjoy a collection of Power Quotes from some of our Ambassadors found in our *Sister to Sister Series*. They contribute insights on how they've been challenged and succeeded while getting to know and show their worth. We hope you resonate with some of these confident and courageous women.

We would also like to introduce you to our little Eva. She's a texter with a bark as big as her bite. What's a day without a bf texting you and hoping for that perfect text line with closure? After all, Eva's got it together and knows and shows her worth.

Inspirations are upon us. You see them everywhere. Celebrities quote them every day on social media or fill entire books with them. Yes, we have a few of our own but we especially want you to know that these were all written for you. You, the woman who wants to know her worth and invest in it every day. We want you to be confident, find the courage to be powerful, be bold, laugh at yourself, and own the world. We wrote these small nuggets of hope and inspiration so you could equate them to some specific part of your life. Enjoy reading them and keep investing in you.

And then there's our Womantoons! Part of knowing our worth is being able to laugh at ourselves! We hope you find one or two that make you smile!

Finally, we want you to know that we love to write books together. But the most fulfilling part of writing a book is writing for someone else. We have written this book for you. We are two sisters from families, communities, and work environments filled with women. We understand there are still many challenges ahead but we can't stop now. We are two sisters within millions of sisters, and we want to encourage all of you to *Know Your Worth, Believe in Your Worth, and Invest in Your Worth*. We expect great things from you. Why? Because *You are Worth it, Girl!*

I dream about...

TAKE OUR
30-Day
Challenge

JESSICA & MARILOU

We challenge you to invest in yourself everyday! Try a new strategy for 30 days!

GOOD LUCK

DAY 1
30-DAY CHALLENGE

COMPLIMENT YOURSELF EVERY HOUR

POP QUIZ

Women are making headway toward gaining CEO positions.

☐ TRUE

☐ FALSE

TRUE: In the latest Fortune 500 list, 33 of the companies on the ranking of highest-growing firms will be led by female CEOs for the first time ever. To be sure, that sum represents a disproportionately small share of the group as a whole; just 6.6%. But it also marks a considerable jump from last year's total of 24, or 4.8% (MPW Fortune 500).

28 PERCENT

OF STEM (SCIENCE, TECH, ENGINEERING, MATH) JOBS ARE HELD BY WOMEN.

When you think you're not the smartest person in the room, but soon find out you are, you know you're in the wrong room.

Ella

Which one will you be?

The difference between a player and a participant is the player knows how to compete with commitment, passion and purpose while setting her sights on winning. The participant will stand aside, watch and wait for the outcome.

We are now

making

Policy

and not coffee!

INVESTMENT TIP

One small action that shouts confidence is the ability to take a compliment. Most women have trouble with something so simple and often deflect praise by saying, "It was nothing." Practice saying, "Thank you."

DAY 2
30-DAY CHALLENGE

GO A WHOLE DAY WITHOUT ALCOHOL OR OTHER SELF MEDICATING SUBSTANCES

I can't control having to be in court for a big case when my kid is having her science fair. I explain this rationally to my little girl. She's smart and I think she understands. I want her to grow up and not experience guilt like I have.

Alexa

A neighbor girl just asked me if I was married and I told her no.

So?

Well, then she asked, "Then who buys all your pretty clothes?"

BE

Bold and speak up

Don't take a job or join a company for what it could be in the future. Don't buy into the story, buy into what the company is now.

Miki

Stop pitting us against one another with these ridiculous, 'Who wore it better?' scenarios in the media. We all look amazing!

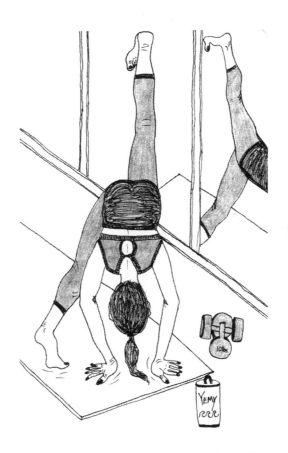

That moment when you realize exercising really does give you a "leg up" in life.

15

DAY 3
30-DAY CHALLENGE

FINISH THAT BOOK YOU STARTED

Women should not be afraid to speak up and ask for things. Start by asking and telling your superiors at work what your goals are and what you want from an early stage in your career.

Beth

Power and influence are elusive.

BUT ONCE A WOMAN HAS IT, SHE CAN FEEL IT IN EVERY INCH OF HER BEING.

I think more women should compliment each other. She looks great but no one is telling her. You never know what someone's going through at the moment. It is so important to support other women in some way. Reaching out to friends and giving them encouragement is the perfect confidence builder.

Finley

HELLO
I AM

CONFIDENT

AND READY FOR
ANYTHING!

INVESTMENT TIP

We all know money doesn't increase one's happiness. But gratitude thinking can! Commit to being grateful for all the good things in your life to strengthen your confidence.

DAY 4
30-DAY CHALLENGE

UPDATE
YOUR
RESUME

When I hear a woman say, "I'm just a teacher, I'm just a mother", I cringe. I am a fierce women's advocate and I try to coach women to be proud of who and what they are.

Anita

74 PERCENT

OF WOMEN SAID THEY THOUGHT THEY WOULD BE MORE WILLING NOW TO SPEAK OUT AGAINST HARASSMENT AS A RESULT OF THE #METOO MOVEMENT.

It's ok to check in with yourself and say, I think I need help. Asking for help doesn't make you weak. It will make you just that much stronger by asking.

Morgan

Snowflakes and women are very similar. No two are ever alike. They can melt in the moment or come together creating intense power among those they surround.

DAY 5
30-DAY CHALLENGE

TRY A WHOLE DAY WITHOUT TURNING ON THE TV

Since girlhood we've been told that nice girls don't brag. Get over it. You need to brag. If you don't brag, or for a better word, self promote, you will become invisible.

Daria

POP QUIZ

Women surpass men in obtaining college degrees.

☐ TRUE

☐ FALSE

TRUE: Fifty years ago, 58% of U.S. college students were men. Today, 56% are women. According to the Pew Research Center, in 2020, for the first time, the share of college-educated women in the U.S. workforce passed the share of college-educated-men.

Your best situations will always come from being uncomfortable.

Lauren

Know your worth, Mom

When you add up all the careers a stay-at-home mom is worth, it's well over $100,000 a year. Think about it. A cook, daycare worker, janitor, laundry attendant, nurse, gardener, taxi driver, teacher and accountant. Don't ever underestimate your worth, Mom!

Regina loved her new job working virtually from home. Her only problem... trying to find the perfect 'Casual Friday' outfit!

INVESTMENT TIP

A crippling fear that prevents women from embracing change is leaving one's comfort zone. Let's face it, change is difficult. Think... in the end do you want to be standing there with nothing accomplished because you feared taking a chance?

DAY 6
30-DAY CHALLENGE

SHOW UP EARLY

I was straightening my hair as an African American woman because that's what we were taught. I didn't realize the message I was sending my daughter.

Lisa

Eva

I just overheard someone calling me a "bitch" in the hallway.

You're a successful and powerful woman leader. People need to get over it.

Express yourself

wear a new shade of

Lipstick

each day of the week.

What inspires me? People who help other people, animals or the environment. I have so much love for people who volunteer. If I was set financially for the rest of my life, I'd dedicate my working days to helping animals.

Beth

DAY 7
30-DAY CHALLENGE

ELIMINATE
WORDS
SUCH AS
"LIKE"
"YOU KNOW"
"UM"
FROM
YOUR
SPEECH

When you walk into a space as a woman of color you must have confidence. I find that I must reflect on how far I've come and know that I'm worthy to be there.

Katy

Girls don't want a break in life

THEY WANT WHAT THEY HAVE ALWAYS DESERVED.

Life

Begins at the end of your comfort zone

While moving up the career ladder I literally changed my own style and wore suits every day thinking they gave me power. They did on some days. But later in my career I learned I could maintain my individuality and dress in ways that still gave me confidence and comfort. It can be a long day in a suit.

Sophia

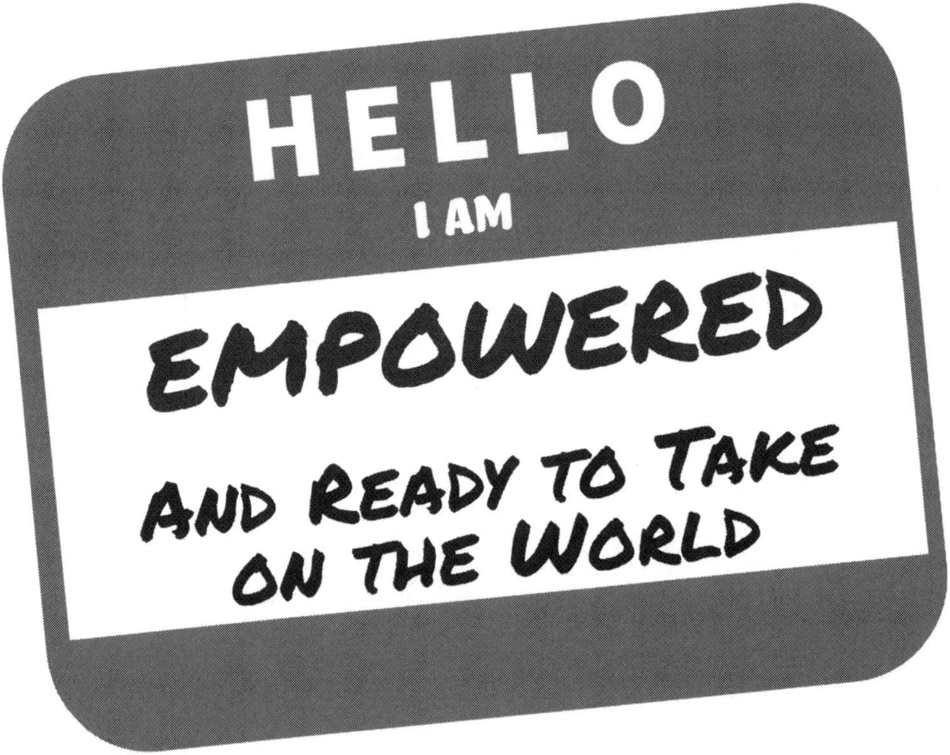
HELLO
I AM
EMPOWERED
AND READY TO TAKE
ON THE WORLD

INVESTMENT TIP

Over 140 million girls in the world
are not in school. When they become
women, they often end up working
for low wages or depend on their
spouses or family for support. Without
an education a woman's future is
limited. Become your best investment
and begin or continue your education.

DAY 8
30-DAY CHALLENGE

INVEST IN SOMETHING JUST FOR YOU

I love my boss. The thing I admire most about her is that when she speaks to me she makes me feel like I'm the only person in the room.

Victoria

14%

OF ACTIVE
U.S. MILITARY
MEMBERS
ARE WOMEN.

I believe that personal growth is non-negotiable. It's all about getting the right tools in our toolbox.

Jamie

It takes a village to raise a child, but it takes a few volunteers to build that village. Volunteer your worth, girl!

Dish or Cone?

Are you the type of woman who orders ice-cream in a dish or a cone? Dish-you are well contained, all-consuming, warm-hearted, neat, and clean. Cone-you are relaxed and easy-going. People seem to melt in your hand when they meet you. You always worry about leaky or drippy rumors in your department and are ready to clean up a sticky mess.

DAY 9
30-DAY CHALLENGE

DON'T
MAKE
YOUR
BED
TODAY

I had to delete my Instagram and Facebook accounts because I would get depressed when I saw friends who looked better than me or were doing such amazing things in life. I was feeling worthless and isolated compared to them.

Janice

POP QUIZ

Women earn more Doctoral Degrees than men.

☐ TRUE

☐ FALSE

TRUE: Women are earning more Doctoral Degrees than men in the U.S. [Infographic]. Out of nearly 80,000 doctoral degrees awarded last year, women earned 41,717 (53% of the total) compared to 37,062 for men (47% of the total).

I've realized there are more important things to life than stressing about work. I want to continue to grow in my career but I believe there are more important things to life than staring at a computer screen all day. We need to take care of ourselves, our health and try to be happy.

Beth

Women are entitled to play sports, officiate sports, coach sports, own sports teams, manage sports teams, cheer for sports, listen to sports and enjoy sports. Thank you, Title IX!

INVESTMENT TIP

Most women in their pursuit of power often stand to lose the very essence of what made them successful in the first place. Try not to confuse overworking with competence. Are there rules that state women must work longer hours than men to appear competent?

DAY 10

30-DAY CHALLENGE

EAT A BIG MAC AND THEN SMILE

My grandmother once asked me if I'd like $10. I didn't want to take her money but really wanted that $10 so I said, "I don't care." She said, "Ok, never mind," and put it back in her wallet. She then gave me a piece of advice I've remembered all my life...If someone offers you something you want or need, take it and say thank you.

Jessica

Wouldn't it be wonderful if the rich, famous and powerful women in the world reached out to support other women?

WHAT A POWERFUL AND TANGLED WEB WE MIGHT WEAVE.

I am very mindful to point out that I was responsible for the success of a project when I have accomplished something on my own.

Jamie

Think of the word 'make-up'

What does it mean to you? A broken relationship reconciled? A face perked up with color and contour? A bed neatly pulled together after a good night's sleep? Or is it simply what you are made up of both inside and out? Find your own brand and makeup of who you are and who you want to be. This is your life and you are in control.

DAY 11
30-DAY CHALLENGE

RUN OR WALK A MILE

I've seen many women try to fit in with the "bro like" culture especially when working on a team. While this sets you up as an equal I think women should try to stand out in this environment.

Beth

83 CENTS

IS THE AMOUNT THAT WOMEN EARN FOR EVERY DOLLAR COMPARED TO MEN.

The best advice I would give a young woman today would be follow your passion and invest in it every day of your life. Know who you are and work off those strengths. Oh yes, then give and get hugs as often as you can.

Alicia

Brita was the mother of three kids and a
corporate executive with a lot on her plate.
She found 'toilet texting' to be her best
time saver ever.

Roses are red

Violets are blue.

He wants that job

But so do you!

INVESTMENT TIP

Gender studies are clear on the double standard that when women speak and act like their male colleagues they are shunned. This perception has not changed in 100 years. Take time to learn the subtle skills of assertiveness, a critical skill for women.

DAY 12
30-DAY CHALLENGE

CHECK IN ON A CO-WORKER

I think it's important to not
automatically defer to your
coworker just because he's a man.
Don't let them jump ahead of you
to volunteer for something. Be
loud and show your voice because
sometimes it can't be heard.

Lucy

Eva

I didn't get the job. They gave it to a man with no experience.

Try harder. It's tough out there. Don't give up.

I still think it's not fair.

Forget Your Purpose

Sometimes it's peaceful to coast in the moment and forget our purpose. Sailing back into the harbor is a comfort that navigates us comfortably to the dock and anchors us back to our purpose.

Finding grass that's greener on the other side may take more paint than you expected. Keep adding to your palette until you find the right shade of green.

DAY 13
30-DAY CHALLENGE

PURGE USELESS PHOTOS ON YOUR PHONE

We can't be thinking about the past all the time. We must move forward to be better people to each other and ourselves. If it becomes a female versus male world, it's going to retaliate and that's not going to be productive.

Shay

POP QUIZ

Women spend a lot of time on their personal appearance.

☐ TRUE

☐ FALSE

TRUE: Women spend an average of 55 minutes every day working on their appearance. Let's break that down a little further: That amounts to 335 hours every year - or an entire two-week vacation - lost to their looks, according to the TODAY/AOL Ideal to Real Body Image Survey.

Don't

Defer

HELLO
I AM

WORTHY

AND NOT AFRAID
TO CHANGE

INVESTMENT TIP

Grudges protect people from the hurt and vulnerability they feel. Hanging on to the hurt can be a power chip in a relationship. Grudges have a corrosive affect on one's health. Give up the idea that the other person must apologize. You control your emotions not them.

DAY 14
30-DAY CHALLENGE

JOIN
A
WOMEN'S
GROUP

It's very easy to showcase the best part of your life on social media. You try to look beautiful in every post. I find that it's important to pick up your head and come back to yourself. It's easy to get distracted by that piece.

Shay

We all deserve to be at the table. We're all amazing in our own right!

STOP LOOKING AT EACH OTHER'S NAME TAG. WE'RE ALL IN THIS TOGETHER!

When that OMG, terrifying moment of texting
remorse wakes you up in the morning wondering
what you may have sent out the night before!

For me, when working with males, and maybe it's just the age we live in, but I always feel like I must prove myself. I'm learning to know my own worth and not always think I need to do better.

Rose

DAY 15
30-DAY CHALLENGE

MENTOR SOMEONE SPECIAL

Take time to learn about
finance and understand money.
You hear about women whose
husbands die and they don't
know where they are financially.
I think, "Are you kidding? "

Irene

Eva

Did you hear the trend is to give your daughter a unisex name so they will be seen as equal?

That's a great idea. What are you going to name yours?

Frederick

21 PERCENT

OF INVENTORS ARE WOMEN.
OVER THE YEARS WOMEN HAVE PATENTED
DISPOSABLE DIAPERS, PAPER BAGS, NON-REFLECTIVE
GLASS, THE FOOT-PEDAL
TRASH CAN, THE DISHWASHER, AND THE
WINDSHIELD WIPER.

How many of us regret the saying, Children should be seen and not heard? Don't squash little girls who want to be heard. Give them their voice- they will need it someday.

INVESTMENT TIP

Negative self-talk, from "I'm just a secretary or stay-at-home Mom," to "I'm not good at math," are self-defeating and should be avoided at all costs. You are special whatever your role or talents are, so own it! Be proud of who you are and never underestimate your value.

DAY 16
30-DAY CHALLENGE

DON'T STEP ON THE SCALE

I think there's a certain beauty to women particularly as they age. I don't have a problem looking older. Sometimes it kind of fascinates me. It's our social demands that keep people trying to look young and beautiful.

Sandy

Sometimes other people will not like your truth. That's their problem, not yours.

IT IS YOUR JOB TO LIKE
YOU, NOT EVERYBODY
ELSE'S JOB TO LIKE YOU.

Believe

That "No" is a complete sentence

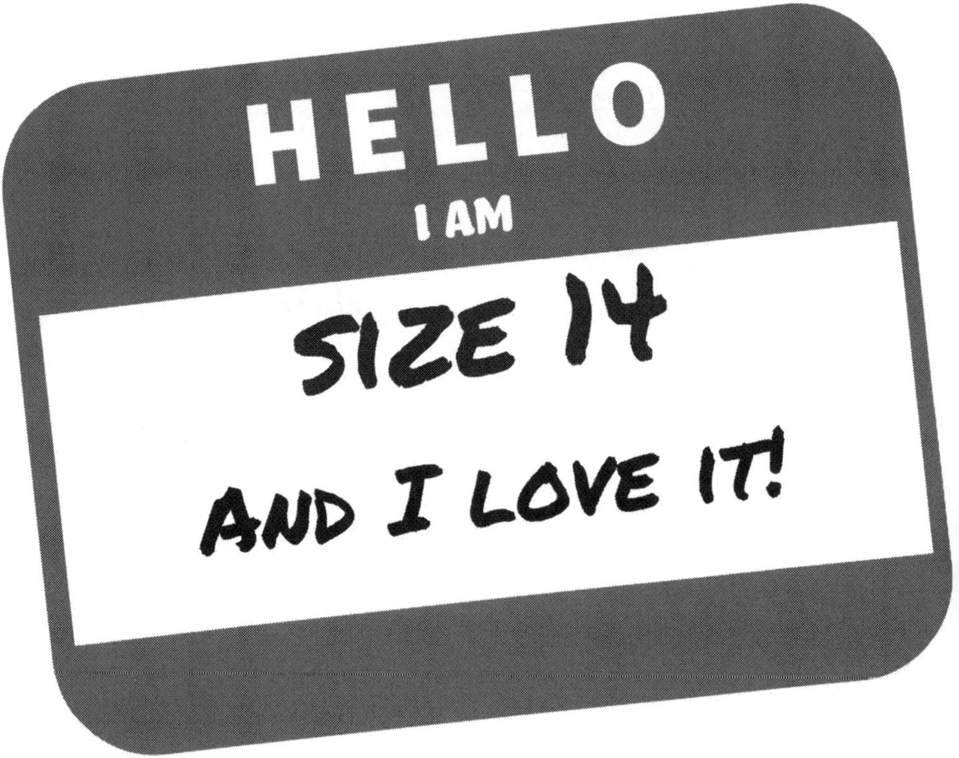
HELLO
I AM
SIZE 14
AND I LOVE IT!

DAY 17
30-DAY CHALLENGE

BUY
A
LOTTERY
TICKET

I think women need to be more forceful in asking for what they're worth and demanding more equality. The time is so right. We are almost at a tipping point where if women would continue to band together we would begin to see the narrative shift.

Sandy

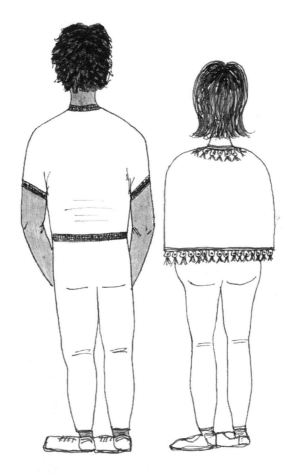

Remember the war between the sexes? Now we just battle over who wore their leggings tighter.

I'm not sure I can do it all. Clean, cook, husband, career and kids.

Yes you can! Just prioritize.

Ok. Career.

Not Fair

Women must take the leadership and forbid men from wearing spandex. It can never happen. It has taken women decades to confidently and comfortably enjoy spandex. Why let men enjoy this privilege without some personal sacrifice? It just wouldn't be fair. Women must pull up, pull in and tighten up this controversial issue.

Don't dwell

on what you didn't do

Yesterday.

Do it today!

INVESTMENT TIP

Most men have no problem looking people in the eye. Women on the other hand, often feel that looking someone in the eye is confrontational and even uncomfortable. Look someone in the eye the next time you speak with them. It can send a message of confidence and power. Try it, it's easy.

DAY 18
30-DAY CHALLENGE

CUT
UP ONE
OF YOUR
CHARGE
CARDS

When I go into a department store the woman working the cosmetic counter would grab me and talk me into a free makeup session. I would walk out of there with over $300 of products. I got smarter along the way and realized these creams would not get rid of my wrinkles.

Shelly

POP QUIZ

Attending a Women's Conference increases a woman's chance for promotion.

☐ TRUE

☐ FALSE

TRUE: According to a recent Harvard Business Review study, attending a women's conference has a real, measurable effect on a woman's career. The data says that in the year after connecting with peers at a Conference for Women, the likelihood of receiving a promotion more than doubled.

Unfortunately, we may never compare to men in terms of physical strength but we can always gain empowerment through our minds. I don't think it's the women who need to do the most to drive change. Rather, the men need to adapt to our power.

Beth

Healing your heart after a bad relationship is like cutting off all your hair. It takes time but when it grows back it will be beautiful and stronger.

DAY 19
30-DAY CHALLENGE

GO
WITHOUT
ANY
MAKEUP

I got fired from an executive position and was devastated. I later learned that I was not listening very well to people. I always thought I was a good listener but my close friends shared that I was the one doing all the talking. Now I try to listen before jumping in with my ideas.

Summer

You've got to know who you are and what it is you want.

YOU CAN'T BE ERRATIC AND SCATTERED. YOU'VE GOT TO HAVE A STRONG SENSE OF MINDFULNESS.

"

When do people ever talk about gaining confidence? I mean, no one teaches confidence, we just expect that you're going to learn it on your own. It's like riding a bike. You're going to fall off. The more things you try out in life the more you fall, the more confidence you will get.

Katy

INVESTMENT TIP

Studies report that most women will only apply for a job when they feel they have 100% of the required qualifications. Men, however, will apply for the same job while meeting only 50%. Perfectionism is not healthy. It's important to know the difference between doing one's best and that of being perfect. Try, "pretty good."

DAY 20
30-DAY CHALLENGE

LEAVE A BIGGER TIP

Don't depend on anyone else to oversee your finances for you. When I was a young girl, my mother sat all of us girls down in the family and said, "Whatever you do in your life do not allow anyone to handle your finances whether you get married or not. Handle your own finances."

Barb

Jackie was experiencing intense "office withdrawal" while working from home. Well known for her creative problem-solving skills, she designed her own snack station.

10 MILLION

BUSINESSES ARE OWNED BY
WOMEN GENERATING
1.4 TRILLION
DOLLARS IN RECEIPTS.

When I go out, I make sure everything looks good on me so there's not something a person can pick apart. We all know there are people out there that are going to look at you and pick you apart so I just take that off the table.

Katy

DAY 21
30-DAY CHALLENGE

BUY
YOURSELF
SOME
FLOWERS

One thing I do to work on my self confidence is to be proud of the small wins. Even if that means going further on your run or being proud of a conversation you had with people in upper management.

Shay

Even if there's rejection, you've got to want it bad enough to keep going. Fall down, get up.

TRUST THE PEOPLE IN YOUR SUPPORT SYSTEM TO HELP YOU OVERCOME OBSTACLES.

Did you hear the men's locker room has a giant flat screen TV, a bar and a popcorn machine?

Don't even go there. Wait, what?

Maybe they'll trade the popcorn machine for our feminine hygiene machine.

Kids are Hard

The challenges of being a working mother or a mother in general is that kids are hard. They don't come with a manual and every single one of them is different. Create your own manual and write the chapters as they come.

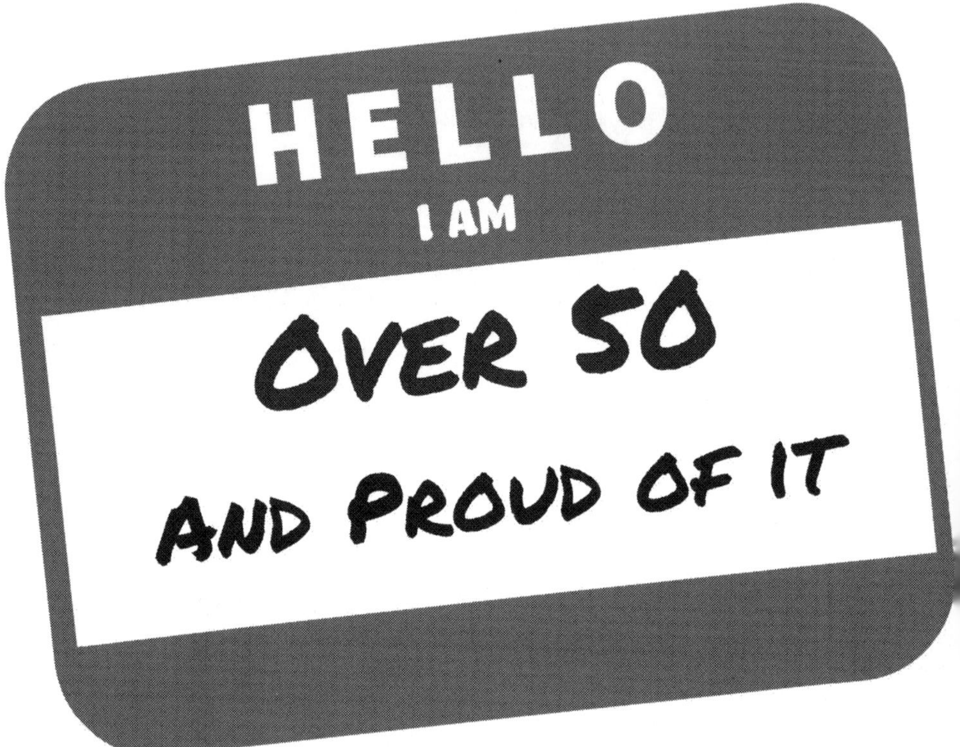
HELLO
I AM
OVER 50
AND PROUD OF IT

INVESTMENT TIP

Authenticity is the number one trait admired by people. Listening with authenticity is one way to gain admiration and trust. Listen to a person as if they are the only person in the room. Look them in the eye, nod your head in agreement, and ask clarifying questions. And SMILE.

DAY 22

30-DAY CHALLENGE

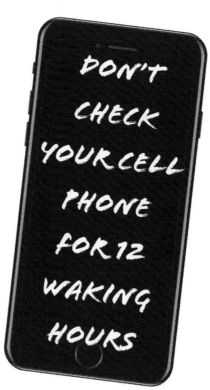

DON'T CHECK YOUR CELL PHONE FOR 12 WAKING HOURS

It took a long time to accept when others were getting boyfriends or getting married and having kids. It takes confidence and knowing there's someone out there for you. You don't need to rush the process. It's better not to force yourself into something that's not going to be good for you and wait for something that is.

Finley

POP QUIZ

Women interview better than men in a job interview.

☐ *TRUE*

☐ *FALSE*

TRUE: Several studies suggest that women handle the stress of a job interview better than men. While women get more freaked out beforehand about the actual interview, we do better in the actual event. Why? Because we research the job and prepare more before the interview.

Here's the thing. Don't treat other women like the enemy. People are going to try to divide us and come between us. We're in this together. No one knows the trials and tribulations of being a woman better than us. We must depend on one another and be able to say, "I need to talk to my sister over here."

Katy

Did you ever stop and think about the time you told yourself four years ago you wanted to go to college? Just think, had you started back then, you'd be a graduate today.

INVESTMENT TIP

Punctuality is the #1 skill rated by CEOs across America. People have a huge respect for punctuality as it signals that you are on top of things, organized and can be trusted. It also communicates that you value others and yourself. Time's a wasting!

DAY 23
30-DAY CHALLENGE

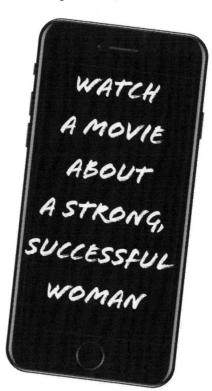

WATCH
A MOVIE
ABOUT
A STRONG,
SUCCESSFUL
WOMAN

Rita wished she'd begged off that "Botox Special" right before her virtual job interview. Now if she could only locate Zoom's secret check-off box she heard about called, 'Touch Up My Appearance'.

You don't choose your family, you're just born into it and there are times when your family can disappoint you. But you can choose your friends. So, it's cool when you can relate to someone and have so much in common. Someone you can trust, push you, and boost up your confidence. I am very lucky to have that in my life.

Laurie

Men are attentive to every move a woman makes.

HOW A WOMAN CROSSES HER LEGS IS THE MOST NOTED BEHAVIOR AND ONE THAT CAN SEND MIXED SIGNALS.

I'm so impressed. How do you always find time for yourself?

The weekend is all mine. I call it Selfish Satisfaction time.

Hey, can you send me a selfie when you're satisfied?

136

"

I've learned to embrace what I call the word "flawsome". I am flawed, but I am still no less awesome. I've learned to accept that there are certain things about me and they are what they are. That doesn't make me a bad mother, a bad wife, a bad anything.

Lisa

"

DAY 24
30-DAY CHALLENGE

MAKE
CONTACT
WITH
AN
OLD
FRIEND

Friday is that time when you're cuddling with everybody and laughing and watching some TV. It's really nice to look down and think, this is my world. These are the little human beings I created. I hope that I'm making this time magical for them.

Lisa

POP QUIZ

Women who volunteer reap huge benefits.

☐ *TRUE*

☐ *FALSE*

TRUE: From lowering stress to boosting self-confidence, volunteering offers many health benefits, such as decreasing depression, staying active, and meeting new people. And there is evidence that suggests volunteering may even help you live longer.

I found it easier to compete with men in the work environment because I think I have a level up from playing sports. As an athlete I was able to demonstrate leadership qualities which now gives me confidence.

Lucy

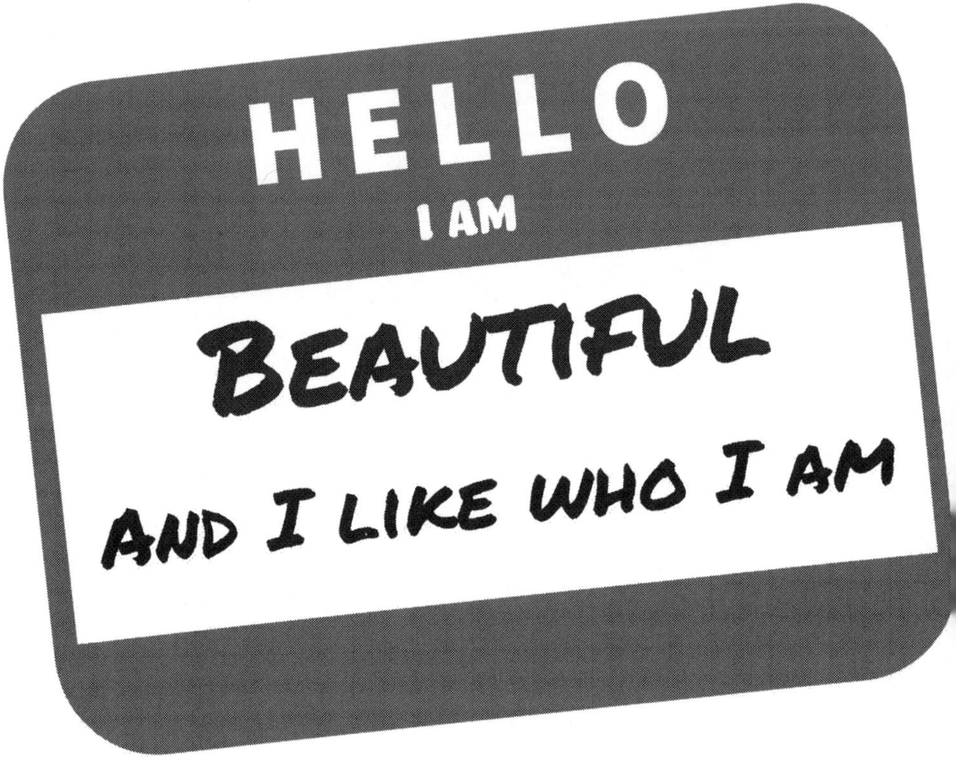
HELLO
I AM
BEAUTIFUL
AND I LIKE WHO I AM

INVESTMENT TIP

An alarming study revealed that 58% of workplace bullies are women and they bully women 90% of the time. If you encounter a bully in the workplace remember there's safety in numbers. Find women allies and build strong and supportive networks.

DAY 25
30-DAY CHALLENGE

THINK "PRETTY GOOD" OVER "PERFECT"

When men are at the top they find men at the bottom with shared commonalities. That's the biggest challenge for women right now. Men tend to promote other men. It's beginning to shift somewhat in that some organizations are gender agnostic and want to hire the best person and sometimes that person is female.

Ericka

70 PERCENT

OF MOTHERS WITH CHILDREN **UNDER 18 PARTICIPATE** IN THE LABOR FORCE, WITH OVER 75 PERCENT EMPLOYED FULL-TIME.

Eva

I'm dying here. I don't know how much longer I can work these 12-hour days.

Wow! Men don't do that.

I love you too!

147

Shannon loved her "Sunday Bottomless Brunches"
which were always followed up with her resourceful
"Tuck-it-in-Mondays".

Hold those Tears

Unfortunately, many men will see crying in the workplace as a weakness. Build up the strength from an early stage in your career and channel that energy into sticking up for yourself and staying strong.

DAY 26
30-DAY CHALLENGE

LIMIT SAYING F*CK OR SH*T FOR ONE DAY

A key conversation I had with one of my mentors was how to manage asking for a pay raise and a promotion. That's a hard conversation. I've only done it once but asking others how they've done it and how to approach the situation helped me put it all into perspective.

Shay

POP QUIZ

Women have always supported women's equality.

☐ TRUE

☐ FALSE

FALSE: Women opposed their own right to vote in 1920. And many Americans remain confused by women who still oppose the Equal Rights Amendment which would guarantee equal rights regardless of sex. The time has never been better for American women. We need to support one another as never before.

Eva

I'm so tired of all these relationships I've been in.

I know but think of all the great stuff you've accumulated from these guys.

You're right. I could open up my own consignment shop $$$.

INVESTMENT TIP

Negotiating salary isn't easy. We must be bold to ask for what we are worth. Seek out a mentor to prepare you for knowing the right way to ask. Believe in the value you bring to an organization. It's unlikely that you'll regret asking for higher pay.

They say it's a glass ceiling. Yes, and a new decade. Well starting in 2020 the glass ceiling is made of cellophane and easily penetrable.

INVESTMENT TIP

Are you a woman who needs to set personal boundaries and learn to say "no" once in a while without feeling guilty? We are often our own worst enemies and take on almost any task with a smile. Dare to say "NO".

DAY 27

30-DAY CHALLENGE

TELL SOMEONE YOU LOVE THEM

For me, as a woman of color it's all about taking things off the table. Get my Bachelor's degree, that's off the table. Get your Master's degree, that's off the table. Excuse me. You don't have a Doctorate? Well guess what? That's off the table. The more you take off the table, the less people tend to judge you.

Katy

Be Your Own CEO

CEO OF YOUR MIND AND BODY

> As a woman working in the trades, I think men should be more involved to get the word out that we can do this job and support us. If we had men who did this then the other men would think it's not that bad for a woman to be working in the trades. There are still guys who think we shouldn't be there.

Corinda

Are you Ready?

All your life you've played with balls... soccer balls, lacrosse balls, tether balls, basketballs, softballs, footballs, volleyballs, nerf balls, golf balls! Now it's time to get some balls and kick ass!

DAY 28
30-DAY CHALLENGE

GO ONE DAY WITHOUT COMPLAINING ABOUT ANYTHING

Ericka was pleased! The "blow up doll" she ordered looked exactly like her. She was sure that her kids wouldn't notice her absence at their games.

65 WOMEN

AS OF MARCH 2020 HAVE **FLOWN IN SPACE,** INCLUDING COSMONAUTS, ASTRONAUTS, PAYLOAD SPECIALISTS, AND SPACE STATION PARTICIPANTS.

I just lowered my golf handicap to 12.5. What's your handicap now?

My husband!

Hey, didn't we agree to no husband shaming?

165

INVESTMENT TIP

When you compare your wealth, possessions, skills, achievements, and attributes to others you can experience envy which makes you feel bad. Be super mindful that envy isn't helpful. Everyone is running their own race and life isn't a competition.

DAY 29

30-DAY CHALLENGE

WEAR ANY COLOR EXCEPT BLACK, GREY, BEIGE OR WHITE

I was beating myself up because I was missing my son's baseball game. How dare you, I thought. You're the worst mom. This kid's going to hate you because you missed his game. Mind you, he's six and has 22 games. But in that moment, I was hard on myself but I knew enough to say, Whoa, stop it, what's going on? He's going to be fine. It's one game.

Katy

Be Done with the Humble Brag.

WE'RE ALLOWED TO
PROCLAIM OUR
POWER.

My boss just told me I needed to talk less and listen more.

Good advice! Run with it.

Look Up

Today, everybody is so
consumed with their phones
and social media. We must
remember to look up and
absorb our surroundings.
Look up, be mindful and
take it all in. It's like traveling.
See the world!

INVESTMENT TIP

A "bad hair" day can leave you feeling self-conscious and down in the dumps. One of the best investments a woman can make is to find a good haircut and then work with someone you trust to regularly manage the style for you. Investing in a good haircut will make you feel better about yourself so that you can be more confident in all of your other endeavors, both professional and personal.

DAY 30
30-DAY CHALLENGE

LOOK IN THE MIRROR AND SAY, "YOU'RE BEAUTIFUL"

Do something that scares you.

EVERYDAY.

I feel guilty having to tell my bestie I can't go to Cabo next weekend.

Hey, I'm your best friend.

Guilt is such a bitch. So is being broke. But I'm learning how to say 'No'.

Get fuming mad. Okay. Get negative. Not okay.

Take the Test

Wake up each morning and see how long you can exist without your social media. Track how long you resisted for 7 days. Evaluate your results and determine whether you felt better or worse for your efforts. Challenge your friends and share your results.

We hope you enjoyed our book!

your receipt.

Confidence	$$$
Courage	$$$
Power	$$$
	Priceless

**invest
in
yourself
and
reap
the rewards**

Enjoy our Sister to Sister Series
www.sistertosister.com

Don't
Forget
Your
Lipstick,
Girl

SISTER to SISTER SECRETS
for Gaining
CONFIDENCE, COURAGE, and POWER

DR. MARILOU RYDER
JESSICA THOMPSON
AUTHORS OF
Don't Forget Your Sweater, Girl

DR. MARILOU RYDER
author of The SeXX Factor
JESSICA THOMPSON

Don't Forget
Your Sweater, Girl

SISTER to SISTER SECRETS
FOR AGING WITH
PURPOSE and HUMOR

Made in the USA
Las Vegas, NV
02 June 2022

49667447R00105